A World of Wonders

Prayers and Pictures
By Robert Cooper

To my wife, Phillipa, and to our children,
Kat, Si and Tim – the four greatest wonders of my world

 CHURCH

Church Publishing Incorporated, New York

A catalog record for this book is available from
the Library of Congress

ISBN 0-89869-434-5

Church Publishing Incorporated
445 Fifth Avenue
New York, NY 10016
www.churchpublishing.org

1 3 5 4 2

Designed and illustrated by Monica Capoferri
Printed in Singapore

Introduction

There are lots of ways to pray. Some people kneel down, put their hands together, close their eyes and talk to God. I like to pray when I am walking round with my eyes open. I also like to pray by touching things with my hands or by tasting them with my tongue. Sometimes I don't use words at all. I watch and listen and try to be aware that I live in a world of wonder and of how wonderful it is to be alive.

I think that prayer is a way of looking at the world. When I pray, I see how beautiful the world can be and also how sad. Prayer is sharing this with God. I can be happy or sad, excited, fed up or bored – it doesn't matter. I can be with God however I feel. I can say anything I need to, even when it's angry or horrid.

Each of us needs to find our own way of praying. Making pictures with my camera is something that helps me. It opens my eyes to see just how full of wonders the world is. By sharing what I enjoy with you, I hope that you will begin to look for your own exciting and special way to pray.

Robert Cooper

This morning, God,
it felt amazing
to be alive!
The flowers seemed to think so too.
Their petals danced in the breeze
as if they were shaking with laughter.
Dewdrops winked in the sunlight.
They looked like tears of joy.
May all the world wake up
to a wonderful day.
Amen.

I couldn't help noticing, God,
how pleased he looks with life!
Is it because he's just had
a new spiked haircut?
Or is he proud of his double chin?
But I can laugh!
With my bobbly nose
and my ten fat toes,
I'd look just as funny to him!
Thank you, God,
for helping me to see
the funny side of life.
Amen.

'Keep out!', said the wire.
The shredded plastic bags
crackled in the wind.
The cone rocked, ready to fall
on someone's head.
But above it all, the sun shone
and puffs of clouds
raced each other
across the bright sky.
Just when everything
seemed as bad as could be,
thank you, God,
for something good
to think about.
Amen.

Green is such a cool
and peaceful colour, God.
Thank you
for making so much of it!
Amen.

I looked
and I couldn't believe
my eyes!
I had thought that
every flower would be the same.
But each had
its own pattern,
like a fingerprint.
Thank you, God,
for letting us all
be different.
Amen.

How still and quiet it is, God!
Only the sun is moving,
rising gently in the sky.
Soon the workers will come
and engines will roar into life.
The cranes will swing
and the river will hum with traffic.
Bless all the world's workers
as they begin another day.
Amen.

Thank you, God,
for spring,
when nature
is bursting with new life.
Seeing this tiny tree,
reaching up so strongly
for the light
made me feel glad
just to be alive
and growing!
Amen.

Thank you, God, for summer.
There is time
to listen to the wind,
to feel the roughness
of the rocks,
to cool my toes in the water.
Summertime is a good time
for seeing
all the wonderful things
that are always close around.
Amen.

Thank you, God, for autumn.
Fallen leaves scrunch
under my feet.
Bonfire smoke
floats on the damp air.
As fireworks burst and blaze
in the night sky,
I warm my cold insides
with a hot dog
and watch the great moon,
butter yellow in the evening sky!
Thank you, God, for autumn!
Amen.

Thank you, God,
for winter.
Today, the melting snow
left behind
this tiny drop of water,
a memory of snowballs
and laughter,
a memory
of smiling faces.
Thank you, God.
Amen.

Looking out of the window
at the storm,
I was fed up with the rain.
But afterwards, outside,
I saw the car,
glistening wet in the evening light.
I watched the clouds
scudding across the windscreen.
It was like having
my very own cinema!
Thank you, God, for showing me
that rain is beautiful
as well as useful.
Amen.

I've just been thinking, God!
My body is nearly all water.
So why don't I pour away
like a river?
The tiny bit of me
that isn't water
must be very wonderful
to keep me
from just melting away!
Thank you, God.
Amen.

The bonfire
pops and crackles
in patterns of leaping colours.
I see pictures in the flames.
Thank you, God,
for times to sit and think.
Amen.

*U*nkind words
are like thorns.
They stab and prick.
Today, God,
please help me
not to say cruel things
that get under people's skin.
Amen.

Thank you, God,
for skilful hands,
for hands that shape
and make.
Thank you, God,
for gentle hands,
that work
for your love's sake.
Amen.

I've been thinking about
these old stones, God.
What wind and weather
they must have seen,
but how beautiful
they have become with age.
As time goes by,
help me to become
more thoughtful, generous
and kind.
Amen.

I'm feeling angry, God.
Inside I'm all boiling up
like a volcano.
I want to explode!
On days like this, God,
I need good friends
to help me let my anger out
without hurting people.
I need real friends,
who will understand my anger,
but still like me.
Amen.

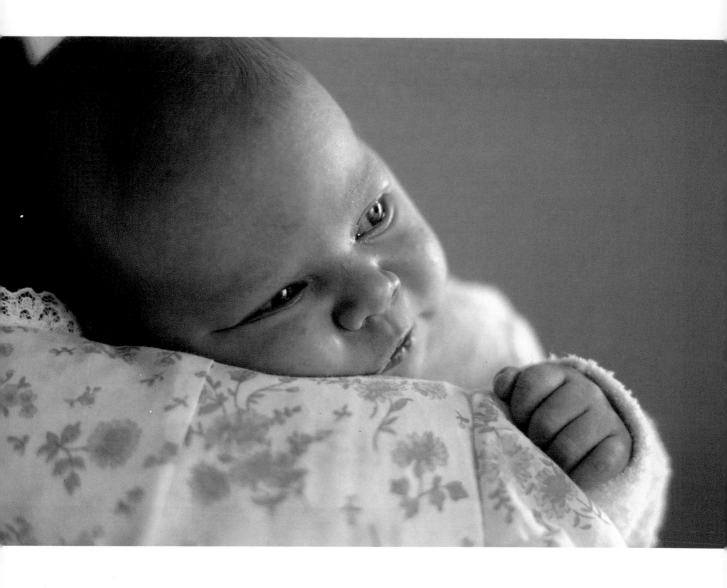

Dear God,
it's good to get up close;
to see the light
in someone's smiling eyes;
to have my hair stroked
and feel the softness of their cheek.
Sometimes, God,
it's nice to know
that someone loves me.
Amen.

$\mathcal{D}$ear God,
here's my birthday wish.
Please may everyone
with a birthday
have a happy day!
Amen.

Dark, stormy clouds.
Glistening sunlight.
How wonderful
they look together!
Thank you, God,
for acts of kindness
that have shone like sunlight
when I've felt
sad and down.
Amen.

 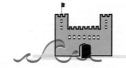 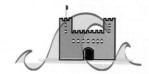

It makes me glad, God,
that sometimes
people really care for wildlife.
I wish everyone did.
Amen.

Dear God,
every day someone's life
is changing.
They can't be sure
what is coming next.
There will be
new friends to make,
new places to learn about.
It's exciting and worrying
all at the same time.
Dear God, please help
everyone who is moving on.
Amen.

$\mathcal{A}$CKNOWLEDGEMENTS

This book was not my idea – it was my wife Philippa's. It was she who also showed my first visualizations to her class at William Cassidi Church of England School, Stillington, County Durham. The children's response, and that of other teachers, encouraged me to take the idea a stage further. I owe them all, but her in particular, a great debt of thanks. I am grateful also to the Revd Mike Raynard, former Adviser in Children's Work in the Diocese of Durham, whose comments on the first draft were both expert and invaluable. Last, but by no means least, thanks are due to SPCK for their willingness to publish this book. In particular I have appreciated the encouragement and advice I have received from Alison Barr, the commissioning editor, and the work of Monica Capoferri, who was responsible both for the design and for the delightful illustrations.